WOLVES OF THE WORLD

Wolves Discovery Library

Lynn M. Stone

The Rourke Book Company, Inc.
Vero Beach, Florida 32964

PHOTO CREDITS
© Lynn M. Stone: cover, title page,
p.4, 6, 8, 10, 11, 12, 15, 16, 18, 21.
© L. David Mech: p.7

EDITORIAL SERVICES
Penworthy Learning Systems

Library of Congress Cataloging-in-Publication Data

Stone, Lynn M.
    Wolves of the world / Lynn Stone.
        p. cm. — (Wolves discovery library)
    Summary: Describes some of the different sub-species of wolves that can be
found around the world.
    ISBN 1-55916-244-9
    1. Wolves—Juvenile literature. [1. Wolves.] I. Title.

QL737.C22 S773 2000
599.773—dc21
                                                            00-020874

Printed in the USA

CONTENTS

GRAY WOLVES AND WILD DOGS

The gray wolf is the largest member of the dog family. Several **species**, or kinds, of wild dogs live throughout much of the world. Foxes, jackals, the raccoon dog, the bush dog, the African hunting dog, and the coyote are some of the wolf's cousins.

Scientists call dogs **canids**. Among canids, the gray wolf's closest cousins are jackals, coyotes, red wolves, and **domestic**, or tame, dogs.

All canids are alike in many ways. They have sharp teeth for eating meat. Most are long-legged for running and chasing **prey**, the animals they eat.

Largest of wild dogs, wolves are powerful runners. Largest wolf on record weighed 175 pounds (79 kilograms).

Red wolf of southeastern United States has some rust-colored fur. The red wolf is midway in size between typical coyote and gray wolf.

Big, white wolves of Arctic Canada are commonly called Arctic wolves. They are one of several subspecies, or types, of gray wolves.

The canids have long muzzles, deep chests, upright ears, and dull claws.

When people talk about wolves, they usually mean gray wolves. Scientists know the gray wolf as *Canis lupus*. The gray wolves of the eastern North American forests are called timber wolves. The small gray wolves of the Southwest are **lobos**, or Mexican wolves.

Wolves live in some 40 countries, including India, China, and Russia. Scientists call the diferent types of gray wolves **subspecies**. They differ in size, color, and the shape of ears.

Mexican wolf, or lobo, is an endangered subspecies of gray wolf. No lobos remain in Mexico, but several live in New Mexico.

Wolves come in many different fur coats. The color of a wolf doesn't tell to which subspecies it belongs.

Arctic foxes are among the wolf's canid cousins.
Foxes sometimes feed on the scraps of an
animal that wolves have killed.

The black-backed jackal is a small canid of Africa. This one and its mate (not in picture) have killed a gazelle in Kenya.

Northern wolves have more rounded ears than subspecies to the south. Wolves of northern areas are larger than gray wolves of warmer regions. For example, the big gray wolves of northern North America usually weigh 80 to 120 pounds (36–55 kg). Wolves of eastern Canada and the Great Lakes states are smaller.

NORTH AMERICAN WOLVES

Most wolf **researchers** divide the gray wolves of North America into five subspecies: northwestern, Arctic, midland, eastern timber, and Mexican.

The Mexican gray wolf, or lobo, is highly **endangered**. It is in danger of becoming **extinct**, or disappearing forever.

The U.S. Fish and Wildlife Service has been trying to help save the Mexican wolf. In 1998 the Wildlife Service began releasing the wolves in New Mexico. Some were killed by angry ranchers. They were afraid the wolves would kill sheep and cattle.

The red wolf is somewhat smaller than the gray wolf, but larger than the coyote.

The few remaining red wolves live in eastern North Carolina at the Alligator River National Wildlife Refuge.

Red wolves are closely related to gray wolves and coyotes. In fact, some scientists believe the red wolf is a mixture of coyote and gray wolf.

COYOTES

The coyote is sometimes called the prairie wolf or brush wolf. During the last 100 years, coyotes have spread from west to east. They are no longer animals of just the western prairies and deserts. Coyotes now live in much of eastern North America, including New York and the New England states.

Coyotes vary in size. The largest coyotes seem to be in the Northeast. Male coyotes range in size from 18 to 44 pounds (8–20 kg).

Coyotes have spread eastward in North America, even into the suburbs of big cities like Minneapolis and Chicago.

This wolverine is feeding on the old carcass of a caribou, killed by a
bigger animal. Wolverines are not a type of wild dog.
They are related to otters, badgers, and skunks.

OTHER WOLVES

Two other animals known commonly as "wolves" were not close cousins of the gray wolf. The Falkland Island wolf was a canid about the size of a coyote. It has been extinct since 1876. Scottish settlers in the Falklands raised sheep. When the Falkland Island wolves began killing their sheep, the settlers poisoned the wolves.

The Tasmanian wolf had a doglike body, but it was not a canid. It was a meat-eating marsupial that lived in Tasmania.

Marsupials are mammals that carry their young in pouches, like kangaroos and koalas. A Tasmanian wolf was last seen in the wild in 1930.

Other canids include the long-legged maned wolf of South America. Maned wolves are not, however, close cousins of the gray wolf.

The Abyssinian wolf has two other common names: Ethiopian wolf and Simien jackal. This canid is about the size of a coyote. Scientists are not sure whether this canid is a jackal or a small type of gray wolf.

Wolves live in a variety of habitats, including the wide-leafed forests of eastern Canada seen here.

The gray wolves of the Middle East act like wolves, but they are the size of coyotes. The Egyptian gray wolf rarely tops 35 pounds (16 kg).

Smaller still was the gray wolf of Japan. It stood just 14 inches (36 cm) high at its shoulders. The Japanese wolf became extinct in 1905. Likewise, the beautiful, white-furred Newfoundland wolf was gone by 1911.

Altogether, seven subspecies of gray wolves have become extinct in the last 100 years.

This cream-colored male wolf belongs to the northwestern subspecies of North American gray wolves

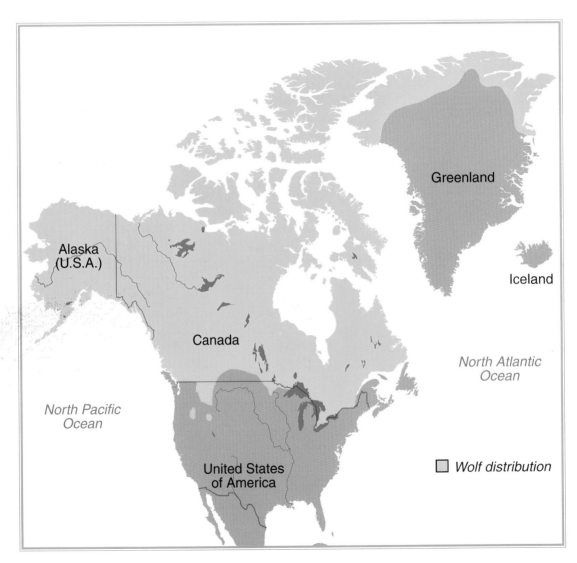

Greenland

Iceland

Alaska
(U.S.A.)

Canada

North Atlantic
Ocean

North Pacific
Ocean

United States
of America

☐ *Wolf distribution*

GLOSSARY

canid (KAY nid) – any of the wild or domestic dogs; a canine

domestic (duh MES tik) – having been raised by people for a long time; of the home or farm

endangered (in DAYN jerd) – in danger of no longer existing; very rare

extinct (ik STINGKT) – no longer existing; referring to an animal whose kind has been completely destroyed

prey (PRAY) – an animal that is hunted for food by another animal

researcher (REE serch er) – one who studies and seeks new knowledge about a subject

species (SPEE sheez) – within a group of closely related animals, such as foxes, one certain type (*red* fox)

subspecies (SUHB spee sheez) – within a species, a slightly different type of same species, such as the *Arctic* and *timber* wolves being subspecies of the gray wolf

FURTHER INFORMATION

Find out more about wolves with these helpful books and websites:

International Wolf Center on line at www.wolf.org

Lawrence, R.D. **Wolves**. Sierra Club, 1990

Patent, Dorothy Hinshaw. **Gray Wolf Red Wolf**. Clarion, 1990

Swinburne, Stephen. **Once a Wolf**. Houghton Mifflin, 1999

INDEX